I0840921

LIBERAL DOUBLETHINK

Rinky-Dink and Pink

by Karen Kellock Ph.D.

A new theory in psychology. According to Koestler, all landmark theories are presented in picture-strip format (right-left integration) to bring on the "aha" experience of the formula (the characteristic of all new paradigms).

FORMULA FOR THEORY:

ALL SUCCESS ATTRACTION
ALL DISEASE OBSTRUCTION
ALL RECOVERY ELIMINATION

The three obstructions are:
people, habit and food.

Remove your obstruction and
you snap to your goals,
waiting in the wings.

LIBERAL DOUBLETHINK

In setting a boundary we may have to burn a bridge. No matter, you'll feel much better.   Having to filter everything thru kings with poor character doesn't sound like America.   He had the charisma to take it to that level but not the character to keep himself there or better. He started out with style--looking good--but quickly became a caricature: a fool or wolf.   War is instructive: losing 95% of the time and then sudden victory: persistence!

THE POWER OF HATRED

HATED FOR BEING CHOSEN
GOD SEES YOU THROUGH ETERNITY
FRIENDS AND FAMILY FAKERY
THEY CAN'T STAND YOU SO GOOD
THEY USE YOU THEN HATE YOU
TREACHERY BROUGHT BOOKWRITING
FROM OVERLOOKED TO OVERBOOKED
STOP TAKING ON NEGATIVE ENERGY
GOD HAS THE LAST SAY
FAMILY & FRIENDS AREN'T HELPING
THEY HATE HOW GOOD YOU'VE BECOME

THE POWER OF HATRED

HATED FOR BEING CHOSEN

The holocaust was the most extreme example of the power of hatred and why we must watch it.

The things I write about day and night are all from those horrible human blights: all so important, aye.

I had no idea how immature my generation was until I let em into my house and what a mess, ouch.

Until I learned **BOUNDARIES** I was invaded by/took on their spirits, taking many years to undo it.

If blessed by God they have their hands out, always borrowing and not returning things, ouch.

They aren't chosen or given gifts/the anointing or blessings but what you have they're wanting.

GOD SEES YOU THROUGH ETERNITY

To God there is no past or future, He sits in eternity. So He saw who you'd be even when a sinner see.

When just a kernel, working things out--the biggest sinner in the family no doubt--you still had clout.

Those persecutions you went thru--being invaded by losers too--all went into your present stew.

God makes all things new and the past is gone forever. It was just a lesson to make you most clever.

THE POWER OF HATRED

It's best to forget the past when you were robbed, manipulated and abused, but it made you shrewd.

You thought your friends & family loved you until you got older. They hate you more now you're bolder.

FRIENDS AND FAMILY FAKERY

If I hadn't gone thru hell with "friends & family" I wouldn't be writing this now, so it's all good see.

God gave me a peculiar anointing to write about human treachery and it all started with lessons early.

Left to our own we'd be great with gifts and anointing til people intervened and made us all crazy.

Why was I such a sinner? Seeking solace to avoid the constant anxiety from people as a beginner.

Sin is a CRUTCH to deal with anxiety as such but then you're just a sick & sad inebriant, out to lunch.

THEY CAN'T STAND YOU SO GOOD

Now you're getting so good they can't stand you. Don't hurt, just understand and continue pursuits.

Everyone loved you at some point cuz God hid your value. But now in full view, be careful Sue.

The better you get the more they hate so never forget: Jealousy is the biggest human characteristic.

Once you showed God you were ready you blossomed like a flower and it was over: careful now girl.

The HERD--any herd--is like crabs in a bucket hating when you get up. Hold your head up chump.

THE POWER OF HATRED

When facing their hate I had to have that drink ok. It's a meat grinder out there: the socialized irate.

This isn't the fifties when there was somewhat decency. It's 2025 and they've never been more crazy.

THEY USE YOU THEN HATE YOU

They'll use you today then hate your guts cuz you got away. Where is gratitude? It doesn't exist ok.

I hate to say it about your fellow earthlings but monsters exist just as the bible says they did.

The nicest among you can become the cruelest when threatened by one getting ahead quick.

The bible says that what they had planned for you will happen to them: isn't God great, amen?

They have their hand out, feeling entitled to your blessings. Don't give it to them, the undeserving!

I felt sickened in my heart when I felt their hate from the start but God gifted me and what a lark!

I turned it all back on em, describing the abhorrent traits of every one of em and what a gift friend!

TREACHERY BROUGHT BOOKWRITING

God said all thru my season of treason: "don't worry, soon you'll tell the truth about their treachery".

I wrote 98 books about those creeps, that's how deeply horrible it was in the ditches they dug for me.

You too may be a late bloomer [since the best traits ripen late] but your blossoming is far greater.

THE POWER OF HATRED

Ain't no more stargazing because YOU are now that star. Doesn't it feel great after going down so far?

They hate you because you made em all out a liar. They told you you'd never be anything, remember?

As you grew up God started showing you different sides of people. You were shocked by their evil.

If you can cut off anyone showing hatred & jealousy and keep your eyes on the prize, you're there see.

If you can cut off ALL who showed hate, by this time next year you'll be rich/one of the GREATS!

God's not hiding your value anymore. This is the thing to remember: you're a target, that's the score.

FROM OVERLOOKED TO OVERBOOKED

You're getting ready to go from overlooked to overbooked. All will do your will even the crooked.

They saw your light and wanted to dim it. They wanted to shut your dreams down so you'd forget it.

Joseph loved his brothers, even when they hated him for his dreams of a future. That's how it is sir.

They overlooked you knowing you were the ONE. Isn't it peculiar about people, can you believe it hon'?

They wouldn't support you like they did their kids, knowing they weren't HALF as talented sis.

They KNEW you were the smartest but showed favoritism to others in the family or class.

They even made it seem like you were STUPID! Maybe the stupidest, the least likely for success.

THE POWER OF HATRED

Be READY for hate, that makes it much easier when it happens. Keep eyes on the prize, fearless.

Now be who God called you to be. Step into that marvelous light: beauty from ashes see.

Be that light surrounded by darkness. But if you're listening to them you'll be part of madness.

STOP TAKING ON NEGATIVE ENERGY

Stop taking on negative energy, feeling overwhelmed. You are the strongest in the spiritual realm.

Anyone who hates what you're becoming is afraid of you. It's over with, go on to new people Sue.

All those years trying to fit in, knowing they hated you. Running from God, your only Champion too.

The minute you cut them off for survival, then they start gossiping about you with both barrels.

You can't care about what they say or feel about you or forget top tier success and breakthrough.

GOD HAS THE LAST SAY

God has the last say over your future and destiny. Not those losers from your past, forget em honey.

Your haters gotta go to judgment day just like you. They'll pay, believe me, so go on and pursue.

Look in the mirror and see the man/woman you've become, how it ALL worked for your good hon'.

When you work in fear & submission to God, you're unstoppable & unbreakable and they're awed!

THE POWER OF HATRED

You can do the unthinkable cuz you're one with God, multi-talented and gifted after called odd!

Your haters won't progress, they'll be in the same place next year. I promise you that so get with it dear.

While they're monitoring and gangstalking you, you have your eyes on the prize, up to the hills, cool.

FAMILY & FRIENDS AREN'T HELPING

You know family/friends aren't helping you. Now that they see who you are that's a sure thing Sue.

ALL your help is now coming from God. He puts one up and the other down so don't look to the flawed.

If they were smarter your haters would realize they're making you greater, and God hates traitors.

The more they lash out with negative energy the more God will elevate you, isn't that great honey?

The more they hate and withhold complements for your success, the greater you are in reaction, alas!

So just because your family & friends hate you never let it stop you. Keep your eyes on the goal Sue.

THEY HATE HOW GOOD YOU'VE BECOME

Just remember, they don't like you cuz you became what they thought you could never be. Now stay free.

Just as an adopted child has bonding issues--turning to any adult as their parent, you may have too.

If you need a friend or prayer, you have me. I've been thru the ringer too and know how to rise see.

GOING NO CONTACT

One can't heal from the narcissist if they're being retraumatized day after day: go no contact ok.

BREAK your thoughts as you would wild horses. It's OUR job to bring em in lest they kill us.

It's too DEGRADING. That's the reason you're getting out of it so remember this always darling.

Be careful because he knows he's a phony and is liable to blow up with the contradiction see.

When the boldly audacious become slow bores you know they want approval from the hordes.

Because I got sicker than the alcoholic they all wanted to blame me for it, that's always how it was.

WE MAL-ADAPTED TO THE SICK

The maladaptive coping mechanisms you use are also making you sick so release him/get on with it.

With time after going no contact your health returns. Enjoyment of life and no more stress/tears.

Curiosity killed the cat so don't go back. That means no more lurking or spying: get a grip.

After time alone you find gratitude and awareness of all your blessings: no more complaining.

What right did a creep have to mess with your mind like that? None, but you loved that alley cat.

Stay no-contact, and you've won. It's as simple as that though it seems so hard at first son.

GOING NO CONTACT

After awhile you feel peace wash over you. After all this it's the best feeling ever, so cool!

Keep this in your thoughts: "The more I avoid the more God fills the void as the trance is destroyed".

It's a direct ratio. The more you stay out the more success comes: keep those thoughts son.

Success does NOT come from east nor west but from God who puts one down/you up as best.

They are nothing-burgers in pant suits and ties. They are pure deception, phoniness and lies.

Don't go there or be degraded, that's what it's all come down to/fated and you must be sick of it.

PROTECT YOUR PETS

King Narcissist always wants to get back--he's vindictive. Guard your pets and fence up.

If he can't kill you he's gonna get your pets. I'm telling you, protect em from this common event.

Don't avoid the light sis. You must be famous to get these extremely important points across.

A grandiose narcissist is a rollercoster: intense bliss and lovin' followed by a massive dose of poison.

Don't show disrespect for God by hanging out with creeps, mockers, losers or insulters: think.

Charisma [emotional skill set] has nothing to do with intelligence--he still sees you as too much.

You're too sophisticated, too cultured, too intelligent and too decent for this flashy gent.

GOING NO CONTACT

You're too forward thinking, too blunt. You're too much of something and there's no adjustment.

False accusastion causes a mix of cortisol and adrenalin, destroying your body like killin'

Intrusive thoughts are Satan's plan to block a destiny so BREAK em son by blocking the nasty.

He can't help but take credit for the good and blame you for the bad, he's a narcissist: sad.

NARCISSISTIC FLAREUPS

He's a narcissist, he will never beg. He'll just move hills and mountains to make you do it instead.

If a man shows sudden outbursts of anger, guard pets. He'll scapegoat em, then they're dead.

Top down hierarchies like the Catholics breed narcissistic flareups enforcing dominance.

Don't read the bible, just listen to the priest. Don't think for yourself but be TOLD what to think see.

Mussolini was a narcissistic flareup but socially driven [same set up] to unify with Nazi thought.

Why else would Catholic countries so readily accept dictators? They adapted to hierarchy sir.

WHAT TO THINK

Don't read bible, read the Book of Mormon. Extra documents are prohibited it said in Revelation.

Don't read bible, read Book of Mormon. Extra documents are prohibited it said in Revelation.

GOING NO CONTACT

Hierarchy [status tension] smashes the self so much he self-protects by becoming a narcissist.

All the energy comes in to protect the self and he can't "see" anything else but his own shell.

TRUST YOUR INSTINCTS

Trust your instincts. If you feel homesicky around some group or guy it's that social evil, aye.

Suddenly I feared, just as I did in Kindergarten around this same milieu of brainwashed peers.

If he's social like them you're gonna have a big problem down the way if you like solitude ma'am.

The odds are your loss if you stay in this race. Why not give it up, turn inside/make an about face?

Why not focus 100% on you & withdraw ALL focus on situations where you're not on the menu?

For we're not all liked 100%. You gonna find your niche and that's where your destiny will present.

Here's where your strength comes in. Overcome any situation by avoiding him & engaging within.

THE FALL OF SELF-WORTH

Recall how far your self-worth fell in like situations. That's how serious this is: AVOID HIM.

God's on your side but you gotta do your part. Any engagement/thought must be blotted out.

He's as bad for you as heroin with his actions affecting your heath and appearance too ma'am.

GOING NO CONTACT

It's a matter of survival. Is this the last battle? No but a major one making you leader of the people.

What is your part? BOUNDARIES. Protecting yourself from evil incursion into your soul honey.

Imagine yourself pierced with ink spreading throughout your system: that's him Ma'am.

Let your last years on earth be happy ones. You know the key now: God's Hedge of Protection.

THE ESTEEMED ARE SLOW

Look around: the esteemed are slow, boring and dumbed but hailed as brilliant/handsome.

You must do this now. What you focus on you become: cut him outa your life/love your home.

Abuse theory: she's abused by her alcoholic. Systems theory: she's part of it and starts him up.

Systems theory: it's cuza her he looks at pornography. Abuse theory: she's assaulted with misery.

Lady: I am not responsible for my husband's drinking or his pornography looking, I'm ok see.

He doesn't love you and talks much to other people while avoiding you so give him up Sue.

He doesn't love you and avoids you while talking to other people so give him up Sue.

I would have done anything to avoid his anger so what could I do but cower in the corner?

When cowering becomes your new strategy it becomes a personality trait bringing hate.

GOING NO CONTACT

Narcissists: a big ego which could crack at any minute--that's why they tenaciously hold onto it.

Their personna is all: their need for continuous approval {supply} the reason for living at all.

Going no-contact includes ALL pc viewing. Never go to his channel if you want true healing.

Get into your own home. The YOU minus HIM: in short time this alights and you'll be in the zone.

APPROVAL GETTING IS EMBARRASSING

He will FALL by conforming to society. With age narcissists get needy and lose their audacity.

It's a very delicate balance between him and the audience and approval-getting is collapse.

All sitcoms have seasons of bad writing and corniness covered by canned audience, it's obvious.

In a desire for approval you'll have seasons of bad writing. Be careful, collapse is embarrassing.

He lost all his audacity in a desire for approval and he collapsed suddenly with a quick removal.

Are you still with him? If so, how is it painfully impacting your HEALTH with all those chemicals?

Cortisol, adrenalin. Weight gain and the blahs, maudlin. Here he comes again, vacillatin'

What I can't stand is false pity & virtue signaling. It makes the bold into a bore and I'm unsubbing.

Life is a phantasmagoria every minute to me and it's all because I went no contact with treachery.

GOING NO CONTACT

If you're gonna treat me like that with comparisons then I'm gone, that's just the way it is hon'.

I was so happily independent and they hated me for it. I would **NOT** adapt to them, the idiots.

They wanted to force it: female slave consciousness. From this came havoc--I feared violence.

DON'T GET SIDETRACKED

Don't get sidetracked into non-issues just because you want something to bitch about Sue.

Choose your battles because there's always something to bitch about but gratitude orders it out.

For every happy minute you avoid him your destiny starts alightin' and success is a-comin'.

The devil is brutal blockage but if it's of God you'll know it: total cordiality, acceptance, help.

RELOCATION FROM "DEMOCRACY"

It's like being in a gas chamber then suddenly getting fresh air. Relocation is bliss: no more cares!

In one narcissistic flareup Mussolini killed 8% of Ethiopia. Tyranny is terrible, see America.

Democracy is two wolves and a chicken deciding what's for dinner. It's horrible and unfair.

Never let "democracy" take over cuz it's cruel. We're a nation of laws not lunacy of the mob too.

We elect democratically but as a nation of laws it's later thru representatives not rule by mob.

SOCIAL TYRANNY

CONSPIRACY AGAINST PRIVACY
WAYLAID BY SENSUAL DESIRE
TALENTS BEFORE GREAT MEN
BORING SOCIAL GENERATION
AFTER THE DISCARD
MANSION CONSCIOUSNESS
LEVEL OF DISGUST = HIGH FENCE
NO ON KNOWS YOUR HISTORY
SATURDAY EVERY DAY
THE BROKEN QUEEN
QUEENS IN THE DARK
MATURE QUEENS
SEEING SIGNS AS SYMBOLS
CAVING INTO ATTACKS
CHALLENGES TO BUILD MUSCLE
NARCISSISM IS FEAR-BASED
CURBING YOUR SPEECH
FASTING IS AMAZING
CALORICALLY DENSE MEALS

SOCIAL TYRANNY

CONSPIRACY AGAINST PRIVACY

There's a conspiracy against privacy in liberal circles. They won't leave you alone: social radicals.

Once revealed he's defaked: a nameless faceless creature with no charisma stark naked.

Invasive and officious, that's what they are. In your face, spying and gossiping ready to war.

These are the devices outlined that hold people down. Some are bad seeds but most are evolved.

Nobody's in your head or know what you went through but they judge it anyway: the human zoo.

A Dionysian, pleasure-seeking spirit made a home in her and diverse sins is an understatement.

Our sins bring on like [dark] reactions but due to anosognosia we think it's their problem.

The queen gets her finances in order so she doesn't have to degrade herself for the rent sir.

WAYLAID BY SENSUAL DESIRE

One can get waylaid by sensual desires and appetites which become patterns: tragic habits, aye.

They saw him as a bum but he was doing something very important for mankind: finding him.

A genius, one of the greatest, can still be blocked or lured into sin--falling into ruin fastest.

LIBERAL
DOUBLETHINK
KAREN KELLOCK

SOCIAL TYRANNY

The queen gets her finances in order so she doesn't have to degrade herself for the rent sir.

One can get waylaid by sensual desires and appetites which become patterns: tragic habits, aye.

TALENTS BEFORE GREAT MEN

Your talents will bring you before great men. That's after a period of solitude/mind expansion.

Instead of viewing homeless videos switch to mansions to quickly upgrade your life projections.

When you think of him now it's like a ghost: a two-faced fickle phony who hurt you most.

They were yelling at you to preserve their fake identity. It's a matter of survival within insanity.

Place yourself inside your mansion videos. Now imagine the insignificance of all your foes.

It's a great mental exercise to use your imagination--a GIFT--as you rise up and the foe falls down.

Relocation--breaking social matrices--is the greatest event but people fear leaving frenemies.

Recover from gutter slime abuse by watching mansion videos while putting yourself there too.

It's not that we wanna live in a mansion, it's about the rich invulnerability to the rabble, amen.

Watching mansion videos uplevels my consciousness so I don't put up with stuff/their guff.

BORING SOCIAL GENERATION

SOCIAL TYRANNY

Man is a theist: We shouldn't deify people but it's a natural if not worshipping God first of all.

You did it: you joined with a bad person without knowing anything about him just to belong.

Another method of intermittent fasting is mouse meals of fat/longer periods of satiety in between.

They bring all their friends to your house. It's so invasive, a groupie thing/all social.

They don't know if you mix or not, they just assume everyone loves everyone and it's nuts.

It's enslavement to give into social expectations DEMANDING you not do what you want.

You find GOD then join a fake church on a treadmill of silly expectations like skits, many heretic.

When women rule the church devolves from pure doctrine to socializing and virtue signaling.

Insofar as women listen to/agree with each other they get weird notions and are inferior thinkers.

Get on solid ground first then talk to women and become good friends. Never adapt to them.

AFTER THE DISCARD

After the discard he gets curious and hoovers back. Be aware of this LAW of narcissism as fact.

After suffering his callous fickleness you don't see him the same way again, more like a ghost.

A queen doesn't get hung up on a narcissist like others with broken consciousness, no way sis.

SOCIAL TYRANNY

You see fickleness, comparisons and minimization and you CUT that soul tie right now, this moment.

For a soul tie is sexual: an issue of self-control of mind and body, of repentance and prayer see.

Since God rescued you from tragedy by you remorsing over the past its unholy ingratitude see.

MANSION CONSCIOUSNESS

A billionaire in a mansion isn't gonna put up with things [like you do on the lower rung]--so ACT hon'.

It's constant distractions rather than facing it all [you acted like an ass hon'] then letting it all go.

Mansion consciousness acts as a barometer that's all, a cure for broken queens and expectations.

If you were a billionaire in a mansion would you put up with these things? Don't do it now please.

Mansion consciousness acts as a barometer that's all--a cure for broken queens vs. the crowd.

Your work is perfect tho' you may not be. Your sins disappear/flee--you're not condemned/free.

Mansion consciousness---total 100% control with a battery of servants to make sure of it: bliss.

It may take decades to undo the damage from force conformity to an image but do it sis.

MLK said the only way to solve racism is treat people based on their character and nothing else.

LEVEL OF DISGUST = HIGH FENCE

SOCIAL TYRANNY

Your level of disgust will determine the height of your fence. Poverty is unprotected/no chance.

The image is you gotta be social but that's a lie and way to a dead soul. I was miserable with y'all.

It's broken consciousness vs. true genius. Get your mansion vision back and discern with it.

With that man you were unequally yoked to an inferior. He bogged you down and made you suffer.

Men don't like being chased and like the male cat will even attack one for invading their space.

Champions: You don't have time to rehash your actions. Act like a pro, go on to the next challenge.

Sensitivity Sux they say. It's what others would be feeling too if they weren't blocked in some way.

NO ON KNOWS YOUR HISTORY

No one knows whatever happened in a ghost town. Let that be how you view your past hon'.

When we grow it's coals of ashes on the abuser's head. That alone shows it's a system instead.

Opponents of the democrats are now labeled "white supremacists" and their color is irrelevant.

I always found social occasions demeaning, triggering and empty. I really hate em so don't ask me.

How they hold em down: by seducing them or traducing them [calumny--killing their reputation].

Nobody remembers a thing about the ghost town because like all of your history, it's gone.

SOCIAL TYRANNY

The dumb in power seek to lockup what they don't understand and you can't argue with that.

The most important thing about the mansion is PROTECTION, not close to the street hon'.

"No man knows my history" said the enlightened superior man. It's true and it's Einsteinian.

Truth for ya: Anorexia does not reflect ego, it reflects TRAUMA and food means momma.

SATURDAY EVERY DAY

I start my weekends on Tuesday because that's when the creativity takes off like a rocket see.

It's Tuesday but for me it's Saturday every day. That's my new life after relocating far far away.

There are those who work and those who smirk. It's doing a Creative Act or self-promotion jerks.

Stop with the guilt/shame torments for after you're gone there is nothing but your achievements.

So what do you wanna do now that prison's in the rear view? Keep it there or return after a few.

THE BROKEN QUEEN

Broken consciousness is the lack of self-awareness allowing one to settle for low standards/less.

The broken queen simply can't accept her God-ordained status because of an empty self-esteem.

When broken she's cemented to a painful past, incapable of embracing a brilliant future alas.

SOCIAL TYRANNY

Broken consciousness positions the woman to be managed by inferiors and the world.

The queen conscious know who they are from soul and spirit. An etched identity--they own it.

Queen consciousness is the high concept independent of other people's opinions: forget all that.

The queen doesn't need the world to cosign her self-esteem. She's the holy God's daughter see.

QUEENS IN THE DARK

I didn't know any better. I sought approval from any direction and caved in totally to insulters.

I suffered if a clerk looked at me funny. Inside I was full of weird nightmares but still totally empty.

I had no self-awareness whatsoever. Get your kids in touch with who they are or it's all over.

I was not only a broken queen but an open book. No one ever told me about users, pedos, crooks.

Life was just life with no meaning whatsoever. I walked around in a cloud punctuated by hunger.

MATURE QUEENS

The queen has the capacity to own her destiny: this is who I AM/this is where I'm GOING see.

The broken queen is STOPPED by the world's purpose to break her down: the self goes underground.

A queen has the inner fortitude to embrace her OWN life and future with faith in her abilities sir.

SOCIAL TYRANNY

You gotta love yourself more than others. You love God, then yourself, then others as yourself sir.

You've loved others more than yourself. Can you love yourself as much as cats/dogs my child?

Poverty's a bit like being in a prison: there's no protection from bullies like being in a home.

What makes man human: seeing signs symbolically and symbols significantly [living shrewdly].

SEEING SIGNS AS SYMBOLS

Seeing signs as symbols, the wife knows her husband's having an affair or viewing porn/evil.

From eyeblinks to posture, something's just off. There's a big deception and it's not of God.

No matter how educated or admired they can still take the sin lure and without the Savior it's over.

Stop remorsing over when devil was the default setting. In that situation anything can happen.

An infinite number of mishaps happen when the devil's in control so exchange ALL of it for gold.

Put that era in the trash to go out. Put all dark events in a bag, throw the whole bag out now.

Be the smart one in the group and be bold. Don't escape em, tell how how to make gold.

They're in a DROUGHT, a mental and spiritual stupor. Selfies aren't a selfix, force em to dig deeper.

CAVING INTO ATTACKS

SOCIAL TYRANNY

Did you cave-in to attacks for all those dry years, or was it a fertile anarchy going on inside dear?

You don't wanna be senile in front of evil. Retire from public eye while still ahead people.

Those people whose opinion matters will be dead like all the others so why give em a thought sir.

You gotta get GOD'S approval cuz he controls and gives all things. Must prove He can trust you see.

That's right, all you gotta do is get God's trust and you're there. Simple isn't it: just get clear.

CHALLENGES TO BUILD MUSCLE

He threw challenges on path all through the journey here but eventually you can rest cuz you're clear.

The kingdom of righteousness, light and Christ can't mix with lawlessness, darkness and idols.

Narcissists are fear-based people. Propping up the false self for survival makes life unreal.

They live with the fear of you toppling their paper empire but they deny it like they know who they are.

With astonishingly low levels of self-awareness and insight, it's all about his image of king/knight.

They live with a pattern of lying. They don't question it while you're in the lurch or regress to spying.

Telling lies is their approach to a fear-based life. Avoiding details, evasiveness, or strife.

He needs to be in control in FEAR of your independence--which is his greatest fear of all sis.

SOCIAL TYRANNY

Women should not invade a male's space. Whether it's a human, a dog or cat you'll be attacked.

NARCISSISM IS FEAR-BASED

He says he has no fear but then intimidates anyone who doesn't buy into his agenda: it's clear.

Narcissists throw threats and can't handle complexity or arguments from anyone who objects.

He can't handle distinctions. You see fine differences like an artist but that's shut down fast.

They justify why their ways are better than yours as they fear differences, even in a princess.

Defensiveness: the main indicator they're fear-based. Vulnerability is impossible in every case.

His anger is his way of shutting you down. Too much complexity brings the nuclear option.

CURBING YOUR SPEECH

You know he's like this so you curb your speech. You become a simpleton to avoid a breach.

He wants you to be more like he wants you to be, like shaking static from a radio. You go low.

It's unnerving/aggravating to a queen to be treated this way: as if she exists to make them happy.

She's not a slut but a traumatized woman with broken boundaries and overrun, a natural reaction.

Emotional or unresolved trauma can bring on shaking or heart attacks and I've felt this in fact.

SOCIAL TYRANNY

There are physical reactions to **EMOTIONAL** trauma and it's age-based with novel symptoms late.

The emotional trauma that's stuck/unresolved comes out in extreme shaking like a blocked valve.

He talked with me about the **EXACT** trauma event, I was able to let it go and the shaking left.

There's no protection from other people if you're poor. Envision the prison yard vs. locked doors.

FASTING IS AMAZING

The best possible thing you could do is **NOT EAT**. For any important event especially/don't cheat.

Just fast all of the time punctuated by mouse meals of fat, like a tab of almond butter in the aft.

A swig of orange juice, a piece of cheese or a sip of the soup cooking--that type of thing.

The extreme emotional pain landed on the eating function and **ALL** her energy locked on.

She was always happy when eating because early trauma was palliated in these feedings.

Then anosognosia sets in: denial of one's condition. There's a blind spot as in all addictions.

At this point I don't eat I graze but not as often as a cow does, maybe every one or two days.

CALORICALLY DENSE MEALS

What is the "right" diet? Reversal Dieting between all of em: this is how knowledge improves lives.

SOCIAL TYRANNY

After months on fruit the fish really woke me up. It's a catalyst as the reversal acts like a shock.

Mono-mania [dieting] is not smart. Paleo man had meat at times but then a berry binge for a lark.

I began eating mouse meals of high quality foods every so often. No more meals and much fastin'.

The one way to withstand fattening aspects of chemicals poured on us is: limit meals or fast.

I need calorically dense food. I tried the sparse--salads and smoothies--but satiety was fleeting.

I want calorically dense so I can go as long as possible between meals: that's the highest people.

So whenever you hit a glitch [boredom, writer's block, inertia] = SWITCH to different hormones quick.

LIBERAL DOUBLETHINK
Rinky-Dink and Pink

WOKE SCHOOL BOARDS
HOW TO MAKE GOLD
BOUNCING BACK AFTER BREAKUP
BROKENNESS AFTER BREAKUP
GO BEAUTIFUL NOT LOW
PUT YOURSELF TOGETHER
FORGET SECOND CHILDHOODS
MEN GOTTA DO DISHES NOW
FEMINIST NARRATIVE MAKES US UNHAPPY
PEOPLE REALLY DON'T CARE
NARCISSISTS ARE VICTIMS
HOLLYWOOD SCUM
AS PREPOSTEROUS AS IT SOUNDS
NEW LIFE AFTER PERSECTUION
THE NARCISSIST
LOWER ARCHETYPES FROM SIN
GROW FROM SEPARATING FROM
THEY'RE ALL ABOUT IMAGE CONTROL
A MATE HAS TO UNDERSTAND YOU
HE'S THE CENTER OF ATTENTION
SUDDEN CATASTROPHE WITH HE/SHE
THEY REVISE HISTORY
DISENGAGEMENT IS BORING
WARNING AGAINST RE-ENSNAREMENT
NATIONALIST POPULISM

LIBERAL DOUBLETHINK

Rinky-Dink and Pink

KALERGI PLAN [ALL BROWN]
EVEN BIDEN SEES SENSE IN FENCE
AMERICANA APOLOGETICS
WE ALL NEED A FENCE
MEN HATE OPEN BORDERS BY DEFINITION
DIVERSE SOCIETIES HARD TO GOVERN
COMMUNISTS WEAPONIZE MINORITIES
MAGA HATS ARE DANGEROUS
LIBERALS ARE ALWAYS GROUPIES
RACE-BAITERS CAN'T BE REACHED
WANT POWER? BRING IN PEOPLE OF COLOR
97 IQ FOR NATIONAL PROGRESS, OR REGRESS
IQ DIFFERENCES BY NATION
ALL CENSORSHIP IS OF POPULIST RIGHT
RICH AND WHITE ARE HATED

Rinky-Dink and Pink

FROM CHARMING TOWNS TO SLUMS
UK IS NOW AN EVIL LAND
CORTEZ THE PRETTY SCUZZ
BOTTOMLESS PIT STRANGE AND BRUTISH
MARGINALIZED BY REPLACEMENTS
TAKE A SIDE TO STAY ALIVE
DEFEAT IS AN ORPHAN SO JUST GET ALONG
THE UTOPIAN ZOMBIE LEFT
VICTIMS ARE THE BIGGEST BULLIES

LIBERAL DOUBLETHINK
Rinky-Dink and Pink

WOMEN REASON LIKE BROADS
IT'S A CRIME TO LOVE COUNTRY
WORLD PEACE THROUGH AMERICAN SUPERIORITY
GO ALONG AND BE GONE
SHARING BRINGS ENVY/TREACHERY
AMERICAN EXCEPTIONALISM GONE?
CRITICIZED BUT REMEMBERED FOR TRUTH
IT'S SEXY TO HATE AMERICA
HATE AMERICA BUT CAN'T WAIT TO GET THERE
YOUR WORK YOUR WAY
DON'T LET EM IN OR SUCCESS BE GONE
GOD GIVES CHALLENGES TO GROW
HIX POLITIX
FRENEMIES
HIPPIES
GO TO PRISON TO LEARN OF FREEDOM
CNN'S FOR "FREE PRESS"
RENEWAL OF CONSERVATISM
FEMINISTS HATE DADDY TRUMP
MAUDLIN MASOCHISM
THE GREEN SALAD MYTH
FRUIT, SUGAR AND STARCH
DISEASE MONGERING
IT'S NOT WORKING
PRESCRIPTION FOR ALL DISEASES
CAMOUFLAGED FASTS

LIBERAL DOUBLETHINK
Rinky-Dink and Pink

Every success story shows two phases: trouble then enjoyment. To get here we had to go thru that.

Relationships with liberals will get you into incredible trouble and below I will show you how.

Eldering consciousness is panoramic view of life as the temporal lobes open to infinity/being high.

Just when you're in your best years--at your crest--they mock you for being old, useless, regressed.

WOKE SCHOOL BOARDS

She started her book with "Republicans suppress votes" and I knew instantly her work was a joke.

Confidence in Biden's ability to ensure quick post-pandemic economic recovery is lowering.

"President" Obama showed a shocking indifference to the plight of a little girl raped in innocence.

A little girl raped and a woke school board trying to cover it up in deference to trans stuff.

The school board attacked father for justified outrage at his daughter's rape passed off as ok.

And then to have the Biden Administration siccing the feds on parents as domestic terrorists!

They're gonna use the FBI to investigate parents going to school board meetings to talk or cry.

A little innocent girl is raped and Barrack Obama says "it's all fake outrage, it's no big thing ok?"

LIBERAL DOUBLETHINK

The school super lied then actually covered up a child rape in order to push woke politics, ok?

HOW TO MAKE GOLD

Being on the Potter's Wheel in the desert wasn't to build strength but to pull back, lessen, constrain.

To heal memory see things eternally: your repentance purifies both the past and the future see.

Part of making gold is the nigredo stage: "no one's as bad as me" but it passes then you're free.

In an instant he went from the dirty old man archetype to the elderly gentleman we all would like.

Anosognosia is when everyone else sees what your problem is but you're in denial/a dam fool.

Look how charming and nice Brian Laundrie looked in their videos--let that be a lesson kiddo.

BOUNCING BACK AFTER BREAKUP

After a breakup we're compromised but with some it haunts them for the rest of their days.

Wisdom is too high for a fool. That's why you couldn't stand em around so get alone, stay cool.

A just man falls seven times and rises up again. Stop bashing self cuz it ruins your soul friend.

Stop holding on to toxic nostalgia: thinking of only the good memories not the horror done to ya.

Obsessing over good things is a broken soul's way of not letting go of the familiar even if harmful.

LIBERAL DOUBLETHINK

A broken soul keeps remembering how he smiled/loved at first as toxic nostalgia blocks the facts.

There's always a way that seems right but the end are ways of death. Inside's a demon, believe this.

Throw a demon out and go to the things or God he'll come back with seven others more strong.

Every time you repeat this cycle it gets harder to break while you become more weak, even a freak.

With breakup immediately enforce a lockdown. Another relationship won't fix a soul that is broken.

You need inner healing, self-discovery and development not to fall back into that old story/bagashit.

BROKENNESS AFTER BREAKUP

One is BROKEN after breakup. Now's the time to be with God not shift into another relationship.

Throw a demon out & go to the things of God or he'll come back with seven others more strong.

You need to recover, you're not fit for a healthy man right now. It takes time: fast, sleep, walk, sew.

You need to fast from relationships for awhile, let God do His healing work so you again smile.

Now your spirit takes dominance not the shattered reality of rejection and broken consciousness.

It's body, mind and spirit [whole] vs. those being out of balance and the FLESH taking control.

Going solo brings yourself into divine order: Fast on relationships so your own spirit is superior.

LIBERAL DOUBLETHINK

This fast gives you your power back: **POWER** over your relational choices & decisions is fantastic.

BE STILL and know that I am God. Be still: don't make wild decisions like sex vacations: grow up.

A broken heart can make you ugly. Don't let yourself go, get into self-improvement to be lovely.

Jolly Jimmy was beloved by his friends but to his wife he was an evil bastard who tortures his woman.

You gotta push back against the normal tendency to let yourself go. Work to be beautiful not fall low.

I was so brokenhearted I wanted to die, It was all in the gut/solar plexus warning me of a cheat's lies.

GO BEAUTIFUL NOT LOW

Don't let a broken heart bring you low. You must fight back with all your might: be bold/beautiful.

Start working out, go on a clean energizing diet, note your daily gains and keep that guy out.

You can be beautiful beyond his new supply of fresh meat. Transcend this clown who cheats.

Meanwhile get close to your God who puts one up as He puts the other down: please only Him!

A broken relationship esp. if sexual can mess you up for life. Attachment trauma kills/causes strife.

Never sink in your swill over a man/woman. Get up, rise up, call on your God who loves **YOU** man!

Get fit and cut: a bright happy ageless sprite. Now he wants you back but too bad you've gotta life.

LIBERAL DOUBLETHINK

The life God wants to give you [minus jerk or Jezebel] will be awesome but not if still hooked doll.

For people are good and bad--all have two sides--and they'll ruin you for life: never confide!

Given the evil nature of man with some good, politics reflects and must block invaders fullabull.

The veneer of "man's goodness" came over us in the sixties, as did relationships ending in tragedy.

It's common with forsaken women: gain all that weight, forget makeup and diet, becoming feminist.

It is not vain to put in the effort to be the best physical version of your godly self. **DO IT** love.

PUT YOURSELF TOGETHER

Get endorphins moving for your new glow. Exercise and eat right to feel good about yourself girl.

PUSH yourself out of depression. Cull your wardrobe, buy new, make your look nice/wholesome.

This will boost your self-esteem instead of lowering your standards due to false depreciation.

You aren't exercising to get another man. No ma'am! It's to recover YOU, God's peculiar darlin'.

You look in the mirror and YOU like what you see. It's about encouraging SELF not a "he".

Snap out of it girl--you in the sweatpants for three days with uncombed hair and the drapes drawn!

You gotta put out the best physical version of yourself cuz YOU gotta look at yourself/the lady elf.

LIBERAL DOUBLETHINK

When all has gone to hell you must encourage yourself in the Lord. No one else: keep this **FIRST.**

Don't do something stupid like a boob job. You don't need melons hanging off your chest/blobs.

FORGET SECOND CHILDHOODS

Don't live a second childhood over this either. You're far more attractive as a lady, mature.

You never shoulda had sex outa marriage. Though encouraged it puts you at a disadvantage.

You gotta put yourself together. No sweatpants and focus on making yourself a star or whatever.

Shut down good memories when they arise--they're a mirage. You got hurt cuz it wasn't of God.

Dressing appropriately for the situation and your self makes it easy to be around you, no?

When you put yourself together others articulate your value unknowingly, don't forget that honey.

From being with a fool telling you no one wants you, you now get complements and love too.

It makes it easier for you to see your own value since you've been degraded/mocked by a fool.

MEN GOTTA DO DISHES NOW

Joan Crawford couldn't see she was a raving lunatic and backstabbing witch especially to her kids.

Traditionally the mothers pass down to the daughters how to keep a man happy but this is gone honey.

LIBERAL DOUBLETHINK

It's not enough for Joe to do the dishes, now he has to **WANT** to do the dishes or she bitches.

He must now intuitively know what is expected and work it into his schedule without objections.

He can't play golf all day anymore, she has him on a short leash. Those dishes gotta be done see.

Leisure time for married men's been shrinking for decades—but if a man supports me he can play all day.

Men are absolutely controlled by what is appropriate behavior from the female point of view sir.

FEMINIST NARRATIVE MAKES US UNHAPPY

The feminist narrative is constantly making everyone unhappy--like the housework tragedy.

Despite his supporting them, the marriage is doomed if he doesn't do enough housework: this is modern.

Women conform to what the feminists say they should want and they are miserable and nuts.

It's always been known that women just want love and a happy home but now that's a syndrome?

You never hear the other side because happy wives don't have a need to bitch, complain and deride.

The language used now in marriage counseling is the opposite to this, it would be the out-thing.

Modern women reading this would go ballistic--they gotta say the politically correct things [fascistic].

Marriage counseling ends up about housework as the therapist takes her side about the jerk.

LIBERAL DOUBLETHINK

There's many reasons she doesn't have sex with him. If he does the dishes he gets laid, amen.

Ecstasy is how my fuse got lit but stay on the other side in those world of lies which to you is legit.

This is pivotal: When they're prospering people will accept strange, cruel, preposterous ideas.

PEOPLE REALLY DON'T CARE

Germans prospered under Hitler in the 30's so many became indifferent to the Jews taken away.

Equity in diversity means: Even though I'm bad at basketball I deserve a place on a major team.

Critical Race theorists work with only one variable: REVENGE--and this desire can't be quenched.

Narcissism is a virus, a raging global pandemic crossing all cultures and invading your immunity.

Youth are five times as likely to be narcissistic--it's exploding in younger generation diagnostic.

In the past people didn't know how to identify narcissism nor how to defend themselves against it.

The Age of Post-Social: Damaged people give up and go inside--they don't interact properly or at all.

The damaged/naive population is prey to the narcissists and that's what it eats/how it spreads fast.

The wild type narcissism occurs in childhood as a result of trauma and abuse, in teens it is worst.

The only reason she comes around at all is to solidify her position and do some damage control.

LIBERAL DOUBLETHINK

The man is now acceptable if he shows his feelings [female] not if he fixes the plumbing [traditional]

Male roles aren't good enough anymore--they must behave like women [feelings] to be superior.

As a woman all I want is a happy home and love. That's just normal but the feminists call it nuts.

A man has sex and forgets about it while the woman's stuck with a trauma bond, neglected.

Sexual attraction is so powerful, soul ties easily develop and they ruin life with the devil's lies.

Be chaste until you're absolutely committed in marriage or it's serial disappointments/never cherished.

NARCISSISTS ARE VICTIMS

A narcissist victimizes you is because he wants company. He's a victim and can't relate to non-victims see.

A victimized narcissist feels at home with his own kind so if you've not a victim soon you'll lose your mind.

He transforms everyone around him into a victim so he can feel at home/be in his comfort zone.

They short the people they're televising to but get fawning coverage from mainstream news.

Luck is residue of good design and chance favors a prepared mind so success comes with time.

A dignified woman knows the difference between high value and high profile, flashy and real.

I'll take a high value man, not a high profile one. I want stability, God, love, consistency, home.

LIBERAL DOUBLETHINK

My whole life is words but this is too much for words so I gotta be mute/stay outa the left brain, a curse.

I just can't because I'm not a jerk. I gotta do what's right because some day I'll be in that position sir.

I feel like I'm being carried in a tidal wave of high intelligence and synchronicity, dear me.

In blue states like California gangs take over small towns and the cops stand down, I was a victim.

The cops won't arrest when they break your windows or kill you dog, the kids get away with it all.

They stayed with a Baptist lady who justified or denied everything they did, creating little criminals.

Ageless: 30 desert years saved me social-adaptive stress except when they came, what a mess.

You sweep me off my feet and I don't know why--do you think it's a dangerous soul tie?

HOLLYWOOD SCUM

Hollywood is better than us: more caring/cultured. That's the BS they shove down our throats, neutered.

Mother earth rapists fly in private jets--an ego defense of rulers to exist within their fractured selves.

Despite platitudinous virtue signaling of celebrities they know deep down they are frauds honey.

To compensate for guilt they demonstrate their compassion by loving ALL illegal immigrants.

They love the mother earth, the ozone layer, Black Lives Matter, socialism, diversity and "color".

LIBERAL DOUBLETHINK

They love the mother earth, the ozone layer, Black Lives Matter/queers, socialism, diversity/color.

Overpaid bullshit actors fighting for solar panels makes it all ok despite perversity/acting like animals.

They see us as racists who deserve our lot whereas they are science supporters fighting earth rapists.

Stop giving support to parasites, cowards and traitors of pop culture. Grow up America/be mature.

AS PREPOSTEROUS AS IT SOUNDS

As preposterous as it all sounds they know the sheep will accept it unquestioningly--they already have.

Inconsistency is hallmark of relationships in trouble. They inch forward then pull back to their bubble.

Inconsistency is lack of focus, interest, courage and clarity but an open heart is an attractive quality.

Mind-Gaming: Once the player captures you they pull away to create addiction, hunger, longing.

Teasing, enticing: messing with your mind. Then strategically pulling away to create longing.

They put little things out to attract you then pull back, it's a game in fact that creates sad sacks.

They hook you as a game. When hot is too hot and cold is too cold you must evacuate or get old.

Narcissism comes from trauma and in juveniles it's from parents, siblings and then the gang.

Tho' severely damaged and traumatized they labeled me crazy, odd, needs to be institutionalized.

LIBERAL DOUBLETHINK

If you're in love you. can't communicate normally so it's best just to stay away and get a hobby.

I was traumatized very early for some reason and knowing exactly what it is is not necessary, just heal hon'.

Why chastity: After the highs of lovebombing and sex it cycles back to heartbreak and loss.

My worse persecutor showed no imagination whatsoever and became a communist I found out later.

NEW LIFE AFTER PERSECTUION

I feel I'm in a new life and it's all cuza you. I'm being carried in a current and the future's in view.

Every day's a miracle cuza you, I don't know how or what or why. Is this the right-brain's holistic view?

It's just one word you said that pissed me off and one word you said that brought me right back.

I feel I'm age seven again living on Palm road. Eldering resembles psychosis/sainthood/infantilization.

Aging or saging? Why fight something that is your apex, the self's highest blend, your work destiny?

I feel I'm age seven again living on Palm road. Eldering resembles psychosis/infantilization/sainthood.

But fortunately I have a savior who wiped the past clean, removed the stain and made me pure again.

Women must stay home. It's a man's world and they can have it--look what happens in war darnit.

That's all I gotta say. I'll be talking more about this, the relief of never using the kitchen again.

LIBERAL DOUBLETHINK

I couldn't take a chance of succumbing to your lovebombing just for sex then reversing.

I learned from previous relationships all I need to know. Pure savagery/treachery/disrespect, a foe.

THE NARCISSIST

They idolize themselves while minimizing you--then everything is filtered thru them first too.

They are the final authority over everything. If you have an opinion they have an agenda so forget it.

This is how it works: suddenly you hate him. You finally see who you're dealing with: pit viper venom.

The narcissist doesn't understand anything not pertaining to him. He won't push his brain to see it man.

Since he couldn't man-up he sunk in his swill and man what a mess as we finally see who he is.

Who you thought was your friend is a dangerous, vile enemy so you go no-contact mode suddenly.

Since WWII we see extreme selfishness. It's all about ME and thus the prevalence of narcissists.

LOWER ARCHETYPES FROM SIN

Thru immorality he takes on the archetype of a pathetic weasel, deflated monster or a dirty old man.

I feel so much better not filtering everything through you acting like a sultan with poor character too.

If he can't MAN UP he'll regress to adolescent fear tactics like brawling or insults--he sunk in his swill folks.

LIBERAL DOUBLETHINK

He resorts to insults and brazen sex comments to get hits and likes but the decent can see the light.

Watch how easily he breaks into insults or brazen sex comments for likes--this is poor character sir.

GROW FROM SEPARATING FROM

We grow by identification with, we self-individualize by separation FROM--no more being put down.

Sometimes in setting a boundary we have to burn a bridge. No matter, you'll feel much better.

WAR is instructive: You can be losing 95% of the time and then suddenly have victory: persistence.

He had the charisma to take it to that level but not the character to keep himself there or better.

Started out with style--looking good--but quickly moved into caricature status of a fool and a wolf.

Having to filter everything thru sultans with poor character: that doesn't sound like America.

The narcissist isn't into learning and growth but only maintaining an image for power they want.

THEY'RE ALL ABOUT IMAGE CONTROL

It's about their IMAGE control not truth, honesty, input from others or personal adjustments.

I used this one incident to trigger and clear out all like incidents of the same class of disrespect.

It's called the Fallen Hero Syndrome and once the down-spiral starts it completes itself to the bottom.

LIBERAL DOUBLETHINK

Our awareness of these processes changes what we're attracted to. We play it out, finding it empty too.

I wanted the glittering thing, got hurt and crashed, healed the trauma and am now properly re-alligned.

If you're a complicated person who is **DEEP** you'll never be satisfied with one who isn't, so **THINK**.

My awareness shifted my attractions suddenly and now I wanted a conscious relationship honey.

If you're deep/complex you want a man who's depth can meet yours but not with a shallow narcissist.

A MATE HAS TO UNDERSTAND YOU

A mate has to understand me and how I think, how and why I live my life and what I do all day long.

The most important thing is boundaries and unfortunately the way we learn them is through hurting.

Relationships can be good but if bad you're living with a pit viper and it's dangerous and sad.

I am not going to get involved with someone who's hurting me all the time to keep me in line.

Someone who is so self-centered he sees no need to push his mind to include me save incidentally.

My high boundaries come from years of tears and adapting to others who couldn't care less.

Having lived in the zone of narcissistic indifference you will feel so free returning to your own highness.

When you know you have power as an individual you can be relaxed enough to be **REAL**, to be **KIND**.

LIBERAL DOUBLETHINK

What a coincidence that you just happen to think exactly like BIG corporations, media and academia!

All this stuff you "believe" in--did you just come up with this or are you a dumbed down conformist?

Now that I'm out from under your spell I feel so much better now. Wow--what a lesson to know.

Did you just "come up with" defunding the police, opening borders and giving amnesty without cease?

Your differences threatens him cuz he's not the center of the universe for a moment, imagine that.

If the narcissist won't push his brain to think beyond him, how could a woman with depth be his friend?

HE'S THE CENTER OF ATTENTION

He needs to be the center of attention at all times or it grits his nerves and you're over the line.

He has such a high and lofty image of his own views it's like yours are irrelevant or he just pooh-poohs.

I feel so grateful to be out from under this beast thinking he's the best so I can just live life with zest.

I could shout for joy and climb the highest mountain now that I'm released from you, a big burden.

Every narcissist who reads this thinks I'm talking about him but it's so prevalent, truth is I really am.

I feel so happy to have returned to prior pillars of emotional support while protected in a fort.

People who really care and know you vs. those who don't and look down their nose/insult you too.

LIBERAL DOUBLETHINK

If what you have is different, it's probably irrelevant--those are thoughts of this great intellect.

If they're so critical of you why do they keep coming back? Cuz it makes em feel superior: fact.

Every time you gripe, whine and complain it feeds them, it's their supply--you need them obviously.

Passive-aggressive anger: Getting the anger out with the least amount of vulnerability--they're sneaky.

Narcissists: Not only can they not be open, they can't access the interior of themselves: closed.

Love me, love my dog. That's an old southern saying meaning: you understand me/accept it all.

There's knowing a person's details vs. knowing his heart and investing in the narcissist just isn't smart.

It's passive-aggressive I fear most, they'll do secret things like take your dog to create stress.

SUDDEN CATASTROPHE WITH HE/SHE

Things going smoothly and suddenly there's catastrophe cuz a passive-aggressive has been busy.

Is everyone a narcissist? In this generation just about--so when we meet a nice guy we're taken aback.

I never met such an arrogant, smug man as you and any attraction was momentary insanity, whew.

Don't waste emotional energy on someone who just isn't going to engage with you--he's no heaven.

Save your emotional energy to engage with healthy people in realness, openness, authenticity.

LIBERAL DOUBLETHINK

Conflict reveals character. How to reveal a narcissist: watch how he responds to conflict sir.

With conflict he goes right into control mode which includes silent treatment, cold like wood.

With conflict they establish their superiority while showing no concern for you certainly.

I was SO drawn to you which turned out to be a trigger for inner demons to be worked through.

Made tense by a self-preservation element inside, he flares up suddenly at little things you said.

It takes very little provocation to reveal his short fuse. Quick accusations/straight to blame, feuds.

They don't wanna feel pinned down so arguments are elusive discussions: skirting issues/confusion.

THEY REVISE HISTORY

They're big on revisionist history. Especially in long-term relationships they'll redefine everything honey.

There's no such thing as no communication. The silent treatment is communicating their disdain hon'

A narcissist is HIGHLY threatened by you thinking different from him, even minor things annoy him.

For these reasons there's no talking with a narcissist during conflict so don't chance it.

I pled with boy 'till face turned blue: Ok I think differently, WHY Is this so threatening to you?

Most youth are narcissistic--they're coping skills are woefully inadequate: touchy and explosive.

LIBERAL DOUBLETHINK

If you think differently you're the enemy and as a stupid moron you deserve their anger and enmity.

They have woundedness they carry and thus they're incapable of engaging with you Miss Yappy.

They're so superior they don't see any reason to engage with you in any productive way on any day.

Dignity, respect and civility are a must Miss. If he doesn't show these characteristics dump him quick.

At times he's nice. Don't get seduced by that for chances are high it won't last and you'll be sad/toast.

By the time he was finally gone--no-contact was ON--I was so relieved/free I felt exhilarated disbelief.

You see, not only are people narcissistic they're lonely and empty so they hang around you honey.

It will feel so good to have straightforward communication and loving attention again hon'.

DISENGAGEMENT IS BORING

You will see the narcissist for the bore he is, never truly engaging and as for you, he was never-seeing.

He's nice for a spell but over time his egocentric mindset rear ups and you'll be down in the dumps.

He doesn't know what he's talking about so reverts to minor things to fill in the slots, it's emptiness.

Don't go in with a narcissist cuz he won't change. These quips aren't for him but so you'll disengage.

That one you thought was the love of your life wasn't it--it's the next one who'll be that: LEGIT.

LIBERAL DOUBLETHINK

He'll be a narcissist till the day he dies, altho' with age he won't be as choosy and be practically "nice".

The reason everything's about the narcissist is because we're all affected and he/she is **DANGEROUS**.

It can be withering solitude or it's exhilarating, joyful, creative solitude away from the rude/cruel.

The same face that entranced you may now disgust you and that's how it works in a **SHIFT** so cool!

WARNING AGAINST RE-ENSNAREMENT

Don't give the devil a chance to re-ensnare you--**DON'T GO BACK**. Anywhere he's at, avoid the rat.

I gotta say it again: Satan will re-ensnare you so you must avoid all contact whether online or not.

Before talking to that narcissist, know your boundaries. You are **YOUR** person, no pressure to change.

When in conflict, think to them: "Watch how a healthy person does this" and then practice calm.

The narcissist is such a shrewd devil the one time you go back to his page he'll ensnare you again, ok?

The narcissist can ruin your life quick. So to enjoy the fruits of a greater America dump the prick.

NATIONALIST POPULISM

Immigration--who's behind it? The same people trying to cover it up.

Anyone with a **US** flag is my friend. We're drawing closer since this last decade of being scammed.

A cuckholded country lets strangers in it's house and it's a disgusting thing done by lush/louse.

LIBERAL DOUBLETHINK

Paradox: The less diverse the area the more they're all for diversity, enigma.

One result of multiculturalism is unsecured borders since that would be mean to the invaders.

Trump showed Theresa Mae how to do Brexit but she wrecked it so the deal's off you twit.

Nationalist populism is here to stay so you just better get used to it. Dr. Steve Turley

KALERGI PLAN [ALL BROWN]

Kalergi Plan: Flood white countries with POCs (people of color) to change demography forever.

Third world cultures don't think the way we do nor have the same IQ and we'll see the results soon.

High immigration = loss of culture.

New level new devil need a higher wall because tho' they know nothing they can still be cruel.

Just because they're dumb doesn't mean harmless, they're dangerous because they're dumb.

It's all about immigration, immigration, immigration. Ann Coulter

These people can do no wrong while the good guy's put away. Innocent men jailed for being white, ok?

RINO republicans pretend they'll do the right thing but once in become democrats stealin' and lyin'.

If you embrace the collapse I hope you bought gold and silver. Metals: the only hedge of the clever.

Praise the Lord while you pass the ammunition. If your foe brings a sword get a bigger one. Jesus

LIBERAL DOUBLETHINK

EVEN BIDEN SEES SENSE IN FENCE

Even Biden sees sense in building fence, he's got a huge expensive one around his beach house.

Yah, Diversity is our Strength but Joe Biden doesn't want it anywhere near his fenced pad.

"Not another foot of wall will be constructed by my administration" except around his own mansion.

Biden breaks the law while protecting himself & family from the results of his lunatic policies.

No one listens to/gives a dam what Joe Biden thinks they just know he stinks while our world tanks.

Our allies don't trust us & our enemies no longer fear us and the blame is on dems/the donkey's ass.

AMERICANA APOLOGETICS

Apologetics: Bidenites adopt Obama policy of apologizing for America wherever they go: sick.

He'd better reestablish deterrents & credibility or we're in for a hellish three years unfortunately.

We hate Biden. It wasn't so bad when he was in hidin' but now we see the ugly old demon.

CRT declares war on United States, it's history and who we are as a people while blaming us as evil.

More Obama B.S.: White people are trying to keep blacks from voting and other nonsense.

Tell everyone you know: we're HAD IT with wokism and the tireless double standard of liberalism.

LIBERAL DOUBLETHINK

Left's economic policy: Americans should spend a lot less/government should spend a lot more.

China & Russia jump on the green train yet are the worst polluters ever [unblamed/given free rein].

The Bidenites offer an ideology of despair and decline. They then say to accept less/don't whine.

Accept less, suck it up and don't whine: that's the democrat narrative while they wine & dine.

The Trump administration was clear, strong and didn't take bullies--gaining world respect, truly.

Biden's "build back better" means "destroy America faster" while what we say is censured.

WE ALL NEED A FENCE

We should all be fenced in. The outer world is evil so you protect your own [family or citizens].

Biden misled Americans on border crisis and is weaponizing the IRS to paw thru our business.

True Americans value freedom and opportunity but "government is the answer" is held by lefties.

Reconciliation/infrastructure package is philosophical: more big gov, climate, causes in the social.

Our green president attends the green conference to ask for oil cuz our renewables won't work.

If you don't play by the left's anti-science rules you're deemed a public health threat and a fool.

The unvaxxed are dangerous bioweapons of Covid 19 they say, abusing that slogan every day.

LIBERAL DOUBLETHINK

We Scottish Highlanders love privacy. We have our estates surrounded by molts, dogs, armory.

When the dollar store becomes the dollar fifty store everything's inflated for good of course.

Creepy Joe has a history of telling stories about himself which aren't true. It's part of the whole stew.

My headaches & bloat went away with the cessation of greens as they're filled with nitrates it seems.

Your bad memories are all due to sin so let the heavenly erasure make you pure & clean again.

Headaches: are you taking greens? Cuz that's what it is: nitrates are not just in luncheon meats.

Buying property I am encountering blocks as jubilance turns to doubt when this crap starts up.

MEN HATE OPEN BORDERS BY DEFINITION

Listen: Since a man's job is to protect his family he'd never be for open borders by definition.

Putin-Trump dyad is wonderful cuz he's a Christian and vicious invaders, he won't let em in.

Putin is a fox, he's so clever. Listen carefully cuz whatever he says, he's saying something else.

Always a sub-text to what the man Putin is saying. Complicated, wow factor, clever, daring.

Savor Putin like a famous chess match.

Ha ha "Yah I know about dossiers" said Putin, the ex-KGB who faked em to discredit disagreers.

Christian vs. Muslim extremists and radicals: How can you compare a tiny few to the many thousands?

"We used to create dossiers" meaning he can send him to a gulog. Ha ha He's as great as Trump.

Putin sees that it's not our laws but secret backdoor behind the scenes agreements with cops.

"In a democracy it should be a court" (Putin) not saying USA has become totalitarian of course.

The center left is sliding in with Marxian fanatics that can't be reasoned with so give up and live.

Exclusionary attitudes increase with demographic change not decrease to accept the strange.

Their stance is: no borders, it's a human right for everyone in the world to immigrate to the US.

Getting the right people in power like Salvini/Kurtz will invoke the true history of Islamic invasion.

DIVERSE SOCIETIES HARD TO GOVERN

Diverse societies are much harder to govern than homogeneous ones, that's obvious hon'

Encroaching diversity quickly changes champagne suburban socialists into republican exclusionists.

Groups are all different, like how they handle the trash--the little things bring the greatest clash.

Increaasingly people of color are changing identity to "white" so census may show a white majority yet.

Racially motivated weaponized altruism has failed.

LIBERAL DOUBLETHINK

South Africa was empty/dry then whites created paradise and blacks said "you stole it, it's mine".

It only goes one way. When whites are majority they give blacks breaks but never the opposite, ok?

"Everyone's the same so bad outcomes due to prejudice/injustice"–false, it's IQ differences.

They're not the same. There are tall races, short races, smart races and dumb races (lame).

Myth of the century: All differences in group outcome are the results of prejudice and bigotry.

Why are blacks poor in Africa? "Cuz the whites stole everything/raped our women" false again.

Radical anti-scientific humanist egalitarianism says: All humans are the same and our friends.

Watch out for this or we're dead Americans: "Everyone's the same, all differences due to racism"

COMMUNISTS WEAPONIZE MINORITIES

Communists weaponizing visible minorities started in 1920's and we see the horrible results today.

It's no ones fault that groups have different levels of intelligence but to deny it is incredulous.

Rather than admit to varying IQ they will drive out/kill the farmers supporting the country too.

So much anger they drive out the greatest workers keeping the country alive/out of danger.

Average South African farmer feeds 2000 people so take out 15,000 farmers = 30 million/no food.

LIBERAL DOUBLETHINK

South African farming is very complicated and average IQ of blacks is <74 and they can't work it.

They see socialism as a magic bullet when all it does is wreck society and then fully destroy it.

Pathological white guilt: We're so sorry we gave the world science, medicine and freedom still!

Whites gave the world medicine so now we're as bad as Genghis Khan? START

Fifty whites murdered each day in South Africa, that's one every 20 minutes/still they lie to ya.

RINOS who hate Trump invaded Iraq for no reason/wouldn't admit the mistake/killed Kadafi as fake.

Hillary's server was a drop box to foreign countries to sell all our secrets to friends or enemies.

MAGA HATS ARE DANGEROUS

America and the free market is sexy and communism sux. Jones, Alex

Africa was dry wasteland until whites made it paradise again then blacks said "you stole it friend".

Ethiopians 63 IQ, Americans 100 IQ and you call that equal you fools?

Wearing a MAGA hat is now dangerous so travel in strong man groups, it's most advantageous.

Us surrender/subsume OUR culture to a worldwide system? You gotta be kiddin'

We're losing our country: when good men stand up they're called racist but we can't back down.

As floods of the third world come in they are taught to hate white people and Trump sees evil.

LIBERAL DOUBLETHINK

This country is worth fighting for so close the back door and the rest deport.

White people must start having babies. Do what the Mormons do: have em 'til God says stop.

We're well on our way to being a third world ghetto country. That's what president said: urgency.

When they come from s-hole countries they bring that environment. Look around you, it's not us.

The invaders have a socialist mentality so they drain the government, are schooled how to do it.

Globalist media gives false impressions that blacks and Hispanics get along like cousins.

Blacks are fighting back being imposed upon, but in Mexico considered second class citizens.

Invaders hate blacks and run em outa their own communities yet blacks still vote for like treacheries.

LIBERALS ARE ALWAYS GROUPIES

They're total groupies. If one wins they all win, if you criticize one they all feel shunned.

You're black and vote democrat for a dirty rat who lets strangers in to make you sad sacks?

Hispanic tribalism: You hit one and they all come after you, always outnumbering the poor few.

Due to Hispanic invasion black people are dying/being forced outa Los Angeles—care about this?

Globalist media won't report Hispanic-Black violence cuz it goes against the multicultural matrix.

LIBERAL DOUBLETHINK

First white flight outa cities now black flight cuz they're scared of the Mexicans, there I said it.

Killing an unknown person is an initiation right and most times he's black in a nightmare fight.

RACE-BAITERS CAN'T BE REACHED

Try to find a black politician and he'll talk thru you or walk off--you can never corner em.

Los Angeles is not diversity it's Mexico.

Ultimate Darwinism: Both liberals and minorities center in cities destroyed by what's coming.

Country folk are better prepared/won't suffer the mass violence and Mad Max of the cities.

Afraid of getting involved with Mexicans cuz if one's mad you're targeted by all their cousins.

Even NBC sees socialists are after your money, will fight you for the crumbs on your table honey

They want you to think whites are the problem and that blacks/Latinos get along: WRONG.

Blacks are being murdered by Mexican gangs and one initiation rite is to kill an unknown.

WANT POWER? BRING IN PEOPLE OF COLOR

Dems: Wherever they want power they bring in the people of color.

White Americans easily used due to their false compassion but in other countries there is none.

It's not about gender/color but what's right or wrong and you have whole groups for the latter.

LIBERAL DOUBLETHINK

Knockout games, robbing/rapes: there's a race war going on but it's one-sided against whites.

Race war against whites is being supported by liberal media, democrats and RINO republicans.

They wanna outnumber white Americans.

In L.A. there's a major war between resident blacks and Mexicans esp the new ones flooding in.

There's third world racist prejudice and they're killing resident blacks in L.A.'s ghetto streets.

Why do they segregate blacks from Mexicans in prisons? Cuza what's happening in L.A. now son.

The democrats have fully embraced Bernie Sanders socialism and Maxine Waters nuttiness.

Zimbabwe went from the breadbasket of Africa to the basket case and now it's happening twice.

There are no successful black nations on earth. Foreign Policy Magazine

What does the caravan of low IQs do to host nations? It is horrifying since IQ determines kindness.

IQ pops of 98 and above all have highly developed nation states. The others, forget it mate.

IQ of 85 and below show poverty and social/institutional dysfunction, thought you should know.

97 IQ FOR NATIONAL PROGRESS, OR REGRESS

An average IQ of 97 is necessary for a nation's success. Black Pidgeon

Latin American invaders have an average IQ of 81--wow what fun, our democracy will be gone.

LIBERAL DOUBLETHINK

Low IQ invaders wouldn't even be eligible for military service in the US and you say we need this?

High IQ nations are breaking as low IQ pops are busting thru Europe cuz they're much crueler.

Europe sees its stable, democratic, low crime, low corruption and wealthy modern society crumble.

Italians are extremely unhappy about the integrationist positions the EU wants them taking.

IQ DIFFERENCES BY NATION

Race differences in IQ explains everything that's happening but we can't talk about it unfortunately.

Americans don't care about Russia so shut up about it.

Ethnic underbelly of kids not raised well knowing nothing but rioting, violence and vandalism.

You can't hate blacks but it's perfectly ok (politically correct) to hate whites.

Let's be kind to them so they be kind to us when a majority: good luck on that false reality.

Deep State fears peace between U.S. and Russia, that explains a lot.

You can't explain how they're wrong cuz low IQ limits the dumb throng.

Britain is losing it's culture due to immigration and it'll never be same if you don't act soon. Trump

Whenever you feel bleak/persecuted think of Tommy or Dinesh rotting in jail/putting up with it.

ALL CENSORSHIP IS OF POPULIST RIGHT

All censorship is geared towards the nationalist populist right and none of it at the leftist blight.

LIBERAL DOUBLETHINK

The Alex Jones ban will fuel populism all over the world, just like when Tommy Robinson got burned.

Liberal politically correct sites are celebrated/right is banned but watch for the Streisand Effect.

Drudge, the most trafficked site in the world gives links to Alex Jones updates: Greatness.

The Alex Jones Ban will fuel us more than ever, it's just what we needed and our good end is near.

We'll talk about Alex Jones Ban so much they will see they CAN'T silence neither AJ or us man.

Cortez: Let's see, what do they want to hear? What kinda person should I be to be most popular?

Politically correct suffer from excess of impulsive compassion for those on bottom/hate the rich.

RICH AND WHITE ARE HATED

Trump Derangement Syndrome is interesting/deep but ramifications are scary with these creeps.

The growing hatred for whites was subliminal but with Trump it mushroomed and we see it now.

Not only is he the hated white he's rich too/even worse he gets the girls and it's just too much sir.

Due to Trump people can finally say what they want to say, not like that commie Obama we hate.

Politicians encourage in-group preference to vote as one but not when it comes to whites/they're done.

Trump gave whites the most powerful thing of all: in-group preference and will to defend themselves.

LIBERAL DOUBLETHINK

Donald Trump encouraged white people to act as a group with their own interests at heart/new.

Anti-white policies of corporate world: affirmative action, thought crimes, liberal youth CEOs.

FROM CHARMING TOWNS TO SLUMS

From charming towns where we all know em to segregated slums where no one speaks/no fun.

Why have confidence in the captain of your ship if she steers in to an iceberg? Socialism has 100% rate of failure.

You don't need a loopy old crank forcing you to walk off the plank.

Replacism: False idea of the insignificance and irrelevance of the thing being replaced, like us.

High taxes de-incentivizes Europeans from births and incentivizes immigrants coming to the west.

Trudeau made ass of himself in India so tried to regain in polls by taking on strong man of America.

Wonderful church but it's made up of people. That's where trouble starts--bible says we're all evil.

Christian vs. Muslim extremists and radicals: How can you compare a tiny few to the many thousands?

UK IS NOW AN EVIL LAND

UK has become an evil land where pedophiles walk free but those reporting on them are in prison.

As London becomes less British it has a higher crime rate/more badness.

Justin Trudeau's a globalist puppet taking mother and father outa all docs and you like this idiot?

LIBERAL DOUBLETHINK

Art of the Deal in North Korea: You're either gonna die in poverty or be rich with great prosperity.

Ocasio-Cortez is not making a good first impression and that is the lasting one.

Ms. Cortez is proudly ignorant and an arrogant liar (grew up in rich suburb not in the Bronx).

Cortez is the poster for opining on issues while knowing nothing about em or making things up.

What scares me: the socialist dumb becoming the majority and no way of explaining to them.

What is big government? A knock at your door. It's clerkism, hierarchies or little creeps with power.

Tyranny doesn't come from distant government but its tentacles which are everywhere you are.

Socialism: the statue of the bureaucrat, man with briefcase--that's where you feel it the most.

One meeting with the briefcase and you're a nutcase cuz you've lost your free will/gov framed.

Papers, papers, papers, you can't do it--knock at the door always looking over shoulder/horror.

Hey--what happened to ISIS? They're gone cuz Trump just told generals to "take care of this"

They complain of white supremacy but all I see is "brown power" signs of La Raza in California.

CORTEZ THE PRETTY SCUZZ

Cortez: "Abolish profit, prisons, cash bail, borders"--with thousands of murders a year, sure!

LIBERAL DOUBLETHINK

Anti-bullying programs keep Muslims kids from assimilating while making American kids accepting.

They travel in groups, we don't--so when the Swedish lady invites him over a gang rape follows.

They travel in groups with a thousand cousins so don't flub up or knock at your door, threatenin'

Unless we get our backs up it's the end of the white race. They're multiplyin'/we're cowering, afraid.

Rapes on young boys is a sudden new phenomenon due to all the immigration from Afghanistan.

We don't just hate foreign practices now we also hate liberalism and what it's done to children.

BOTTOMLESS PIT STRANGE AND BRUTISH

I just feel like we're all gonna be eaten up by a bottomless pit brown cavern, strange and brutish.

Those to the south are just as mean/heartless. Must face it: we were the best/flooded with less.

The Nordish far right has burgeoned and now they're competin' to who can be more isolatin'

New nationalist views on border security, immigration quotas, welfare social benefit recipients.

Have hope--when attitudes change re: immigration, policies like welfare also change/they're gone.

Mass immigration means one thing: our piece of the pie will be much smaller/banished altogether.

What's staring us in the face is mass illegal immigration and them flooding your hometown.

LIBERAL DOUBLETHINK

Undifferentiated empathy is bad not good. You have to think not just feel, thus creating hoods.

Sadiq Khan didn't wreck London he was elected because it was already wrecked. Mark Collett

MARGINALIZED BY REPLACEMENTS

Marginalized by people brought in to replace us. It's a criminal armed invasion and our death.

Rather than establishing own nation they're more comfortable living with us making us feel guilty.

We're a distinct people and not everyone can fit in with ya, what a radical view today in America.

Whether they like it or not, must adapt to the new emerging world order with Trump at the corner.

A RICH time to invest--and not just in metals like silver and gold. Full throttle w/Trump thru God.

Of course we hate that Merkel vermin. She let so many in outa false compassion, that's women.

Feminist illogic: Merkel declares multiculturalism a failure then promptly opens all the borders.

Liberalism: Stop having babies to save resources but then import half the third world to make up for it.

Democrat is no longer the party of the working man but of free stuff. They want socialism and hate Trump.

Globalists made media into royalty--that was the plan--to roll it all out while they put down The Man.

Go to the third world countries you find admirable: they are a hell of evil, a palpable den of devils.

LIBERAL DOUBLETHINK

Everyone has to take a side just to stay alive.

TAKE A SIDE TO STAY ALIVE

The coarsening, roughening, grossification of culture has one answer and that's for you to sequester.

The clear knew The Sopranos would cause violence in families/society--that's social psychology.

To hear little ladies dropping F bombs cuz they watch Sopranos: that's social hypnotism folks.

Speech has become rotten/dirty to be part of a chic club and global plan to cause chaos/debauchery.

They know immorality creates zombies so they sexualize and gross us out through the media constantly.

You fall in love with their performance until you hear their interviews and what disappointments!

As vocabulary constricts they become less expressive with clever words just F bombs: dumbed.

After Sopranos came out people started slapping each other around and speaking crass smut.

Terrifying violence coming from ordinary Joe: that's how societies collapse as they copy more.

Anything which desensitizes, grosses. That's why media is decent to keep society at it's highest

DEFEAT IS AN ORPHAN SO JUST GET ALONG

Victory has a hundred fathers but defeat is an orphan. JFK

They're more angry at Donald Trump's UN speech than Rocketman firing missiles without cease.

LIBERAL DOUBLETHINK

Strong silent types just did what they had to do, they weren't in touch with their feelings/maudlin too.

It is weird and sickening seeing the churches swing left. Ear-ticklers, charlatans, carnal, daft.

Don't call cum-bay-yah hotbeds of iniquity churches. These are witches/pickups/God is disgusted.

Most of the churches Paul called false in his day. Synagogues of Satan, outright heretics, pharisaic.

We have every right to hate the globalists and anyone linked to, in cahoots with or enabling the sadists.

Fake feminists defend Sharia Law.

Coming against power doesn't make you a gangster it makes you a patriot so get that straight.

Islam hates west cuz it's evil, left cuz it's unequal. Islam wants caliphate, left wants communist state.

Making right decisions brings success. But now rich are seen as less and the poor as "victims", blessed.

THE UTOPIAN ZOMBIE LEFT

Sovereignty--borders, language, culture--is now a dirty word to the leftist scum who want us overrun.

To the utopian zombie left, globalism means great food, sights and sounds. But it's hell, a human pound.

Nationalism--loving freedom and sovereignty--is pure Nazism to those fed by slogans and comedy.

Why is it bad not to want home invasion? Sovereignty/privacy is a basic right/need for Americans.

It all started with the idea that "all cultures are alike". Dadburnit you're out of your bloody minds.

LIBERAL DOUBLETHINK

Left will force people on you/call you a bigot. Ban em all and trust God for success: turn on the spigot.

The hippy left wants us to be like a commune. Just leave door open and let em all in, we got room.

VICTIMS ARE THE BIGGEST BULLIES

Victims are the biggest bullies in the world.

He may be crude at times but his big instincts are the right ones and he showed em at the UN.

Madman Theory: Since you don't now what they're gonna do you gotta change game quickly.

It's all so self-evident but not to them who hate Trump so we feel like we're swimming upstream in mud.

Why do they even have that creepy show on--The View--if not to dumb us all down and cause feuds.

Took courage to be a patriot (against global grain) but now when it's accepted you jump on the train?

He's "outrageous, inflammatory"--not nice on the surface but underneath criminals, worst historically.

Ill-gotten gains become a hole in your bucket no matter what you have planned in your budget.

Stop peddling your fiction because only dummies are buying it but they can cause dangerous riots.

WOMEN REASON LIKE BROADS

Most women reason like a broad. Wish they'd shut up cuz it's the contagion of madness with the loud.

Of course we put our own country first--just as all countries should--but the left makes that a curse.

LIBERAL DOUBLETHINK

Earthlings are just busy giving and taking in marriage and leaving everything to their offspring.

Global warming plan: tax you so much for your carbon use you go into poverty and they stay royalty.

Hypocrite Hollywood scum air conditioned the outside of the Emmy's wasting carbon on those bums.

The name of the bill "Dreamers" is meant to bypass your reasoning and give into the schemers.

Ignore what democrats spoke: They don't care about kids it's the votes cuz without em they'd be broke.

Illegals disrespect US law so we're supposed to let em in the military with access to massive weaponry?

When she called Trump a sexist scum I thought she was talking about Bill, I mean President Clinton.

Hillary's third unread memoir shows how little she's self-aware that we've awoken and no one cares.

Pelosi catering to foreign citizens/abandoning American children.

The Hollywood scum insulting Trump have never said one nasty word about ISIS, I kid you not.

Trump told the truth to the crowd of gangsters--I mean the U.N. General Assembly (a world curse).

IT'S A CRIME TO LOVE COUNTRY

They make it a crime to love your own country, to love your own first and to appreciate your true history.

You're supposed to love the global whole and to hell with your own little hole as the greatest they stole.

LIBERAL DOUBLETHINK

If you don't put your own country first you put the globalists first making you lowest/worst/cursed.

Robber Barons created the U.N. not as an instrument of peace but of global corporate colonialism.

The globalists own the fake media who hate Trump cuz he loves America and sees right through ya.

You're not gonna get out are you, you're gonna sit here making 15 million a year, bitching with ingratitude.

Studies show that with prosperity the posterity turns to spoiled rotten snot-nosed entitled scum.

WORLD PEACE THROUGH AMERICAN SUPERIORITY

A time of crisis or cluster of traumas is also a time of quickening so get ready to blast off.

With globalism it's a giant sucking sound but with nationalism you build up the countries all around.

Open up the border and the wage goes from $45 to 15 an hour. Ross Perot

Trump's speech to the UN pits spiraling into decadence after having their globalist view blown to bits.

Left is still chewing on Russia collusion fairytale, crippled by cognitive dissonance and their holy grail.

After Trump speech the left tweets: "he talked about rogue regimes but never once Russia", how silly.

All we've ever cared about is immigration--stop em from coming in!

GO ALONG AND BE GONE

Going along, playing it safe is what's gotten countries historically enslaved.

The U.N. itself is the foreign power.

LIBERAL DOUBLETHINK

The left's wild reaction to Trump's UN speech is even more interesting than the speech itself.

Patriotism: the principals for which we stand. Nationalism: My country right or wrong (that's bad).

Everyone knows that if they fire at us we nuke em for crossing the line--Trump saying it is a "war crime"?

You don't go to the UN and threaten to destroy another nation but our man did it from his high station.

SHARING BRINGS ENVY/TREACHERY

We share our resources/discoveries across the world and what do we get? Jealousy, envy, derision.

AmeriKing: Goodness of our people, the greatness of our way of life, our decency/philanthropy/sharing.

America was the greatest force for good the world had ever seen.

Whatever the issue UN tries to get their hands in our back pocket, wanting to make America pay for it.

In history of UN there has never been a more straightforward criticism of other member states.

Obama explaining to fellow authoritarians at the UN why he couldn't do more: "because of our laws".

The world's dictators would never allow their own people freedoms cuz they wouldn't be elected.

You cannot own your future without basic liberty. The rest of the world doesn't have that, no way.

Liberty/freedom = American exceptionalism.

AMERICAN EXCEPTIONALISM GONE?

LIBERAL DOUBLETHINK

American exceptionalism: It's not that we're better than anybody it's that we have a chance to be.

Out of 330 million enough will pursue excellence so we'll end up with a great place, not by chance.

Trump Truisms, like: "Rocketman's on a suicide mission"! Oh smart man give us more of your jargon.

CRITICIZED BUT REMEMBERED FOR TRUTH

The left adores Cuba and Venezuela--can you imagine that, not caring that they have to live like rats.

It's an undeniable truth that socialism has not been poorly implemented--that's just how you do it.

UN buzzcut: We wouldn't mind the huge dues if it delivered what it's supposed to but it doesn't.

Socialism is the only way dictators can ever accept, facts be damned and no matter how inept.

Best of Trump's greatest speeches: Dictators, bureaucracies and assorted elitists couldn't believe it.

Proud of him: He slammed socialism, targeted rogue regimes, threatened to destroy Rocketman.

Trump is speaking to a room full of socialists/communists and he slammed it all cuz he is the greatest.

Dictators know their people suffer cuz they must build walls to keep em in and political imprisonment.

They believe in Marxism, tho' it's never worked--steeped in leftist liberalism tho' it creates jerks.

IT'S SEXY TO HATE AMERICA

To the left it's sexy to hate America.

LIBERAL DOUBLETHINK

You're just a bunch of slogans--got nothing going on but status climbin' cuz it's liberal tides you're ridin'.

They shoulda learned from seeing socialism's failure when Obama sought to change us forever.

He said not to be afraid cuz we have air superiority and moral certitude and that's all we need dude.

Hey guys, we don't have to have a defensive posture with these little creeps around the world!

THE LIBERAL APPEASERS

The liberal appeasers will say "they're gonna attack, we've had it" while the real men say "I love this!"

In my 30 years in the UN I have never heard a bolder or more courageous speech. Ben Netanyahu

Any enemy of ours is potentially their friend so anything destabilizing us is to them a big plus.

World is not a friendly place and what's always kept the peace is American superiority/lines of normality.

The democrats are not into successful military campaigns cuz to them our military causes only pain.

They always knew our capabilities, just at times our willingness as witnessed with the limpest.

No more saying something without saying it. This was bold clear speech and we still can't believe it.

We have nothing to be ashamed of, why cower in front of the world when we're it's main superpower?

It's so unnecessary for us to constantly apologize and downplay our assets-- all from that ass.

HATE AMERICA BUT CAN'T WAIT TO GET THERE

LIBERAL DOUBLETHINK

They hate America but can't wait to get here.

If an ally you'll be better than you've ever been, but if an enemy you're out and same with our friends.

Tho' millions have been starved and killed, the left thinks it's sexy to love North Korea/hate America.

Foes knew they had nothing to fear under Barrack Obama but plenty with Trump, don't you love it.

If the righteous many do not confront the wicked few then evil will triumph. President Donald Trump

I'd rather have a mortal who slips than a president giving a slick speech while destroying underneath.

It was so bold, so unusual--because it was simply the truth.

This has nothing to do with race but respect for our country and our flag. President Donald Trump

YOUR WORK YOUR WAY

It's a complement to be a Manual not a book. While book is put in library, *Manual* stays on desktop.

After working all day for decades suddenly wake up to fame for that's how it works with greatness.

Stop worrying about success and just prepare for it cuz it'll overtake you as the good book puts it.

Prepare to come out of obscurity. It's a whole new ballgame now: new level, new devils/enemies.

And to think it all came from mere words. Guess they're powerful after all: greatness or a curse.

DON'T LET EM IN OR SUCCESS BE GONE

LIBERAL DOUBLETHINK

You can be the most talented with greatest potential but then *people you let in* blocked it I betcha.

It's your style, your groove. It took years to hone a true talent not political or to be socially approved.

See that music is most superior cuz it doesn't track. TV is just static to your pets, think of that.

Words have power but only if terse. Cut the pork then you will move mountains and come first.

You flub up cuz you try too hard. It's embarrassing and evident that you're not there yet/below par.

GOD GIVES CHALLENGES TO GROW

He gives you something to deal with, a thorn in your side to keep you humble, hopeful, compliant.

It was demons (not you) so leave it at that. Now lean on the promise that: Jesus erased the bad.

I'm flying cuz it took a lifetime of suffering from crossing the line and that's the definition of fine.

I laid it out in whole hoping you could grasp the depth, breadth and urgency to act.

The book is the Lords and it is so clever! He did it, I carried it: now I'll let Him pull the lever.

Stop worrying, we'll make it perfect. This is because we're the angels and you are the Elect.

In a brainwashed population truth won't ring a bell. That is the problem and it's scary as hell.

It's not you anymore, it's your invention. Designed by God you did the work but it's owned by the world.

LIBERAL DOUBLETHINK

Though it's a pick-it-up-anywhere book you don't know the years it took studying the crooked.

Let it go, you had your baby. It took a lifetime but now it's born as the world learns the New Theory.

HIX POLITIX

He's not only bad cuz he's a liar, but cuz he doesn't inspire. Rosie O'Donnell on Donald Trump

I'll scratch you off my list, what an idiot. Thus proving: no lower intellect can ever judge a higher intellect.

Get used to being ignored until that moment you POP into the scene, world.

Don't devolve to attention-getting to compensate for your as-yet-unrecognized genius tho' I know it's frustrating.

It will never end cuz if you don't manage negative stimuli (snowflake yourself) you become more panicked.

Less and less is required to trigger you more and more and you end up controlling everyone/abhorrent.

Pedophilia and racism do not exist. It's only good vs. evil that causes hell-- what the low people pick.

Poisons get in through food and clothes so avoid those but firstly stick to what you know in our Bible.

We took the blame for the whole thing completely forgetting all the slimy things they were doing.

He was a great foil for me. Stark opposites, all his different qualities showed mine by contrast, see?

If one rejects you for your words, then they determine your reality, actions, limits, everything--walk away.

LIBERAL DOUBLETHINK

Rejects you for saying something (crossing her lines) but then she comes back, forget her this time.

Say something wrong, lose friend. They come back like nothing happened but censorship/86ed: drop em.

FRENEMIES

Nagging problem: Flaky associates bring constant disappointments so reject this disrespect.

We're nice until we're not then watch out, nuts.

Lotsa saved people caught up with the devil: broken lives, broken homes, evil.

The problem with masochists is when they meet a real sadist.

Be sin free and life becomes perfect too. Don't expect disaster/failure as in the past (just learning tools).

Don't keep remorsing back to lower levels when you didn't know better and filled with demons/fetters.

Possibly a demon for years because of which you acted out, became maudlin or a lush and a louse.

With experience/time you find what works best (FOR YOU) then expand those while deleting the others.

The new cumbaya church music is shallow, emotional, fleshly, sounds the same and is man-centered.

"Quality worship"--from tingle to tingle, search for greater tingle--praise and worship with co-mingle.

All you can do is repent then do what you do best and forget the rest.

Though past doesn't exist it can still make you sick. Forgive yourself for when used by demons, hick.

Things aren't obvious until they are, so be patient and suddenly they'll see afar.

LIBERAL DOUBLETHINK

Jesse P. said to treat all thoughts as evil, of the devil--don't trust em but be like cats/dogs, living now.

Ain't no big thing to wait for the bell to ring. Until that ring, nothing. Grace Jones

Style/strength can't be faked. You either have it or you don't yet not thru birth but correcting mistakes.

HIPPIES

Go to college with the SJW mob: Come out traumatized with no job.

College traumatized me suddenly. Professors were debauched, hated America, made me think their way.

Trump Derangement Syndrome PART 2: Conservatives feel crazy cuz they lost family over voting this way.

America's coming into it's harvest under Donald Trump, God's anointed. It's payback time: know it.

Obama accused Trump of old political theories as if he were superior destroying America forever.

Great biographies are fascinating--most died in tragedy after magnificent opulence and notoriety.

We're moving legally from "intent" matters to only "consequences" matter-- legal system is in tatters.

Microaggression: any act that makes the listener uncomfortable regardless of the intent?

Don't trust thoughts, they're of the devil and the past is gone/doesn't exist. Be just here now like dogs/cats.

GO TO PRISON TO LEARN OF FREEDOM

LIBERAL DOUBLETHINK

Only one cure for SJWs and college profs: put em in an Iranian prison to learn about tyranny vs. freedom

Not all ideologies are expressions of psychiatric disorder but many are.

First they ignore you then they laugh at you then they fight you then you win. Gandhi.

They've so conditioned people to conform that a thinker is totally out of sync and it makes us sick.

When the wicked rule the people mourn. Trump's made us cool though they're tearing him down.

They're making their move--that's why all this evil stuff is happening--so be patient while Trump removes.

CNN'S FOR "FREE PRESS"

CNN advocates for "free press" then protests we be censored.

Heh, God set em up for the kill by tracking em into the virtual world. Maybe we will win, ya know?

How to stop abuse: You take control of the time he spends with--so he can't disappoint, the louse.

Trumps SMV (Sexual Market Value) is just too high as charming/smart billionaire. They can't stand it/gaps too wide.

Trump tells the bloody truth/unthinkingly while Obama gave em a ruse as a big phony/smilingly.

The press isn't the enemy of the people but the fake news (80%) is. Donald Trump

If we show black-on-white crime the media bans us and it's the same in Europe when Islam stabs us.

These people are evil and they're making their move. Alex Jones

LIBERAL DOUBLETHINK

Liberals: 6 x more likely to steal, 9 x less likely to give but 1000 x more like to *say* they're giving.

When people get weak the first thing they seek is power and there is the devil promising forever.

RENEWAL OF CONSERVATISM

Major mechanism in the renewal of conservatism is: resurgence of the nation state.

What is liberty? The right to tell people what they don't want to hear and remain totally free.

No logic to a demon other than destruction and your ruination so stop remorsing back and just forget him.

Wash this generation off. It's a gritty smelly dark aura of ugly mauve tones and living with it is very rough.

Can't stand hearing the lies anymore. It's too frustrating and why should I be debased by the whore?

California isn't my country anymore and it won't be until I'm dead--and it makes me sad. John Steinbeck

No black in power has ever been able to help the black community but a white man did who they hated.

Whoever has guns has the power. When it's just government it's not a true democracy and a dire hour.

FEMINISTS HATE DADDY TRUMP

Trump has been chosen by God to weed corruption. Open borders means one thing: hostile INVASION.

I will clean up the darkness and usher in the light, for I have America in My Hand. The Lord

LIBERAL DOUBLETHINK

For Christians praying for impeachment/death of our wonderful God-given president: hell swallows em.

The smart say democrats will never see the Whitehouse again. This red tsunami is due to their deep sin.

I'm so thrilled at the morality of our president: 15,000 pedophiles arrested yet the news never reports it.

This is the year of major arrests including Hillary/Obama so get ready for catastrophe/social unrest.

About to have the biggest energy explosion in our history. Big companies are moving back, gladly.

Why do they call him a racist when he's the most non-racist president we've ever had? Makes us mad.

Arrogant liberals always talking about their "rights" but what about their wrongs? Disgusting.

97% of news posts on Donald Trump are negative. Due to constitution, we must put up with it.

It's gonna be a red tsunami nationwide so get ready for major arrests of traitors, crooks and pedophiles.

America's set up right now to be the number one producer of ENERGY in 2019.

Initially Trump was to resume his empire after 4 but after seeing the deep corruption it'll be 8 years.

We're outraged after John McCain's glittering funeral turned into a Trump bashing session.

MAUDLIN MASOCHISM

White people were so sweet with their little pets, roses and other plants. Revive our race, save us yet.

LIBERAL DOUBLETHINK

But we're nice to the point of maudlin masochism as we gladly give what is theirs to rapacious invaders.

In the human species it is insanity to care more about out-group than in-group members.

Pros and cons of multiculturalism: One the one hand more beheadings, on the other interesting cuisine.

Multiculturalism: The first bits are interesting then the returns slow down then the problems, profound.

The traveling couple who said evil didn't exist were then killed by ISIS terrorists.

Wherever masses of humans = massive fecal matter but open border liberals don't care about splatter.

Be aware of social impact of stepping over homeless and their feces while exploring the city. Paris Trip Advisory

Poor Germans and their recent guilt complexes apologizing for everything they say and think/stop this.

Confusion is two parallel news universes and that's why it's like we speak two separate languages.

Socialism is philosophy of failure, creed of ignorance, gospel of envy, whose virtue is equal sharing of misery. Winston Churchill

THE GREEN SALAD MYTH

Confused from headaches I'd think "need more green smoothies" to be in the pink [new age stink].

Greens like kale/spinach cause migraine headaches--that's all I gotta say to raw smoothie addicts.

We think of nitrates in bacon/lunch meats but spinach, kale, dark greens? Headaches, yikes!

LIBERAL DOUBLETHINK

"Eat your greens": no other lie has been repeated so much as these migraines are out to lunch.

Put light greens in smoothies like romaine or butter lettuce, now your headaches will pass.

We've always known luncheon meats are dangerous with nitrates but "healthy" salads are too ok.

"Eat your bitter greens". But they're so poisonous God made em bitter so we'd stay away from them.

FRUIT, SUGAR AND STARCH

People usually don't die from starvation, they die from malnutrition from eating crap all day man.

Simple as pie, no hunger: Smoothie in morning, starch and salad brunch. Fast for dinner/wake up winner.

Two opposing theories in food science: [1] we live on nutrients, fats, proteins or [2] we live on sugar.

We live on SUGAR and it doesn't matter the source. I got this all from the great Durianrider of course.

I know it is a discovery--who decides, them or me? Gotta good start on the new matrix, now I'll take a rest.

DISEASE MONGERING

Disease mongering: first step is to define a disease then establish HUGE profits screening/drugging.

After they define two-thirds of the population of being sick they have a great business, ya think?

Once you stop food poisoning the body spontaneously cures. That's all you gotta do--no drugs sir.

LIBERAL DOUBLETHINK

The body has the innate ability to cure itself. Just stop putting in poisons from the grocery shelf.

Bible shows men who ate wheat and water had excellent health compared to men who ate rich food.

Bible shows wheat and water gave excellent health not seen in men eating rich foods of wealth.

The best athletes [from Kenya] live on starches. That's a fact and these are the most elite sports.

They mistakingly think fats create the "glowing skin". Not true it just creates ugly tissue and cloggin'.

What would make you age overnight like that? It's due to the rich lowcarb diet of Kings/crap.

He keeps touting a lowcarb meat diet as healthy while his pics clearly show he has aged remarkably.

A vet sees health/disease from looks alone. With meat they're better at first but with time, all gone.

Switch to starches and the bowels change, constipation goes away and the skin/hair glows again.

IT'S NOT WORKING

Your diet may be stimulating/tastes so good but honey it's not working. I can see it in your looks, ugly.

A veterinarian just looks at the animal and knows. The superior diet your touting is full of holes.

When overcome with taste trip/urges you lose your vision of reality and so you can't see it honey.

"Vegan" can mean living on potato chips and pepsi. It's not vegan [tho' I am] it's STARCHES we live on.

LIBERAL DOUBLETHINK

Billions of people live on starches, vegan or not. Fruit is naturally an occasional thing then it rots.

Nutrient dense diets of kale and cauliflower don't work either so they add nuts and get even fatter.

Fix white rice every morning, put in frig. Doctor it up with vegetables and sauces then you're fixed.

Lowcarb diets are like the devil: they work at first so you become enamored/ensnared and tell all.

In 1970 they changed the oft-used word STARCHES to "complex carbohydrate" and we got mixed up.

Pack the freezer with frozen fruits and there are your smoothies. Otherwise, white rice please.

How does a kid know to eat "complex carbohydrates"? But he'd know how to eat STARCHES ok.

White rice isn't a rich man's fair, doesn't taste that great, very plain and common--can you do it hon'?

I was silent for years cuz I was damaged and traumatized but now I'm back, reborn and energized.

After all I've been through with people I just wanna be with dogs and cats and I'm never coming back.

PRESCRIPTION FOR ALL DISEASES

Prescription for all diseases: Just say "EAT STARCH" not the difficult words "complex carbohydrates".

A "fruitarian" pulls it of by eating six avocados a day cuz they're a fruit but glycation =skin gets loose.

If I didn't have my six avocados a day--it's gotta be soft, etc--I couldn't have done it just on grapes.

LIBERAL DOUBLETHINK

The glycation from years of that was terrible and now it's gone, what a relief to the sight, avo = devil.

I used avocado as a buffer against emotions. In truth I was emotionally hungry but how'd I know?

After this temporary fast I may go on the starches but in the interim it'll be just juices/perhaps soups.

When God calls you not to eat it's nothing to worry about just enjoy the ride/time you have with the Lord.

It's not milk it's a mammary secretion. It's not eggs it's a chicken menses. It's not meat it's a massacre.

They want me to eat mammary secretions and chicken menses but I just can't even the fishes.

Of course all my cats are here, it's warm when it's with mom. Or cool, whatever, to make it heaven.

A little grape juice is fine but too much makes me sick. This is about frugality and a little just fits.

My whole world opened up when I stopped eating solid food. Digestion relieved/energy/better mood.

If you can't fast just eating less is whatcha call a "camouflaged" fast and it's ok--no judge.

CAMOUFLAGED FASTS

Camouflaged fasts work great too. A fast just means "eating less" actually-- cut back, flow.

I'm much happier not eating/digesting. MUCH happier--it's like a whole new world. Who ever said?

This is why I've always been thin I guess. I hate pulling flesh around, when you walk it jiggles--gross.

We don't need all that clutter in the gut. Why do you think ant-acids are the biggest product?

If I thought meat would give me a total physical reset I'd do it, believe me. I just don't believe it/facts.

Yah popcorn is perfect to have around. Make that in the morning or rice for when you're wantin.

KAREN KELLOCK PH.D.

M.S. Political Science, San Diego State. Ph.D. in Psychology, University of California Irvine. Postdoctoral: UCI School of Medicine, Dept. of Psychiatry [NIMH Grants]. Developed the Debris Theory of Disease, a theory of system pathology in 120 books and 22 textbooks for the general public. The theory has a general formula: All disease is obstruction, all recovery is elimination, all success is attraction. The three obstructions are people, habit and food. Remove obstruction and snap to your goals, waiting in the wings.